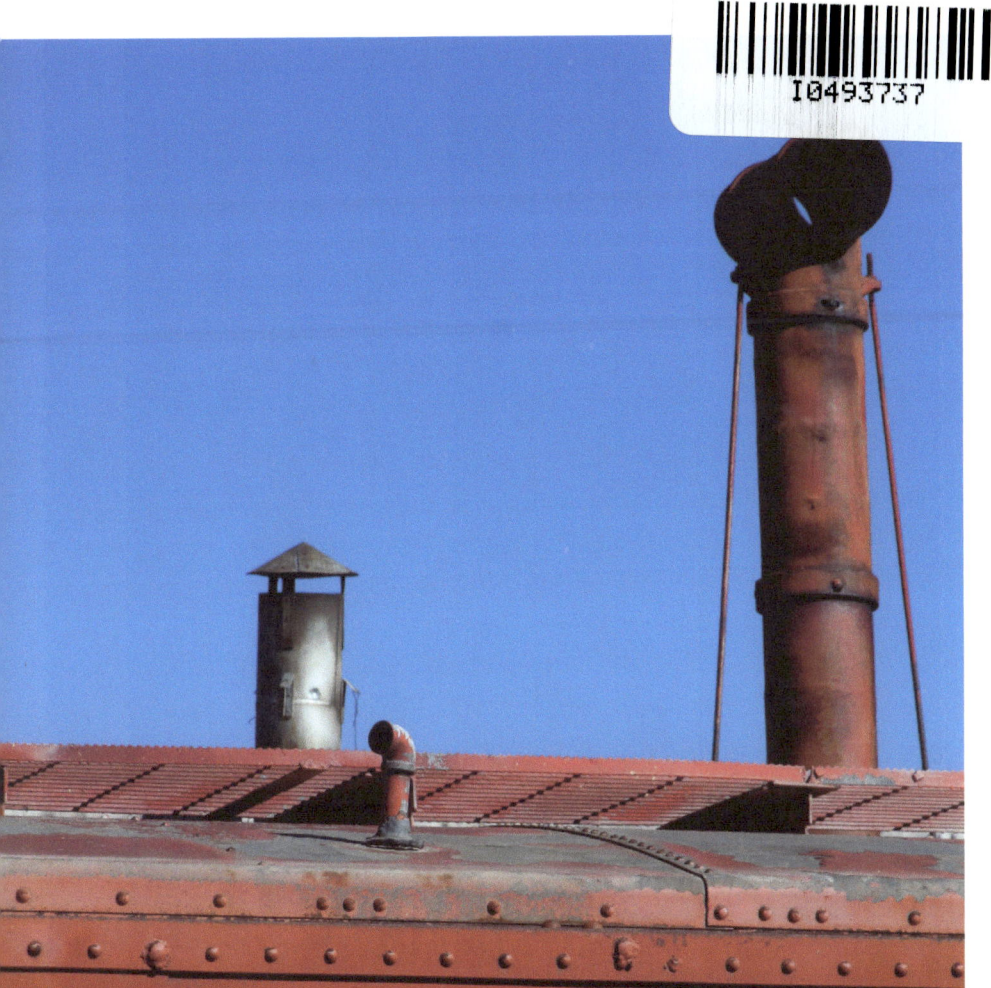

A Mark Dahle Portfolio

Finding Joel

Mark Dahle Portfolios can be read in a few minutes and enjoyed for a lifetime.

This portfolio includes an autobiographical account about finding Joel, a photo of a beautiful 36 x 24 inch painting (at the right) and twenty-eight outstanding photographs from Santa Fe and Albuquerque, New Mexico.

Unlike many picture books, the text is unrelated to the art. This might seem weird at first. One thing that helps is to order more portfolios until you get used to it.

Photographs in this book are available in limited editions. See http://www.MarkDahle.com for more information and for previews of upcoming portfolios.

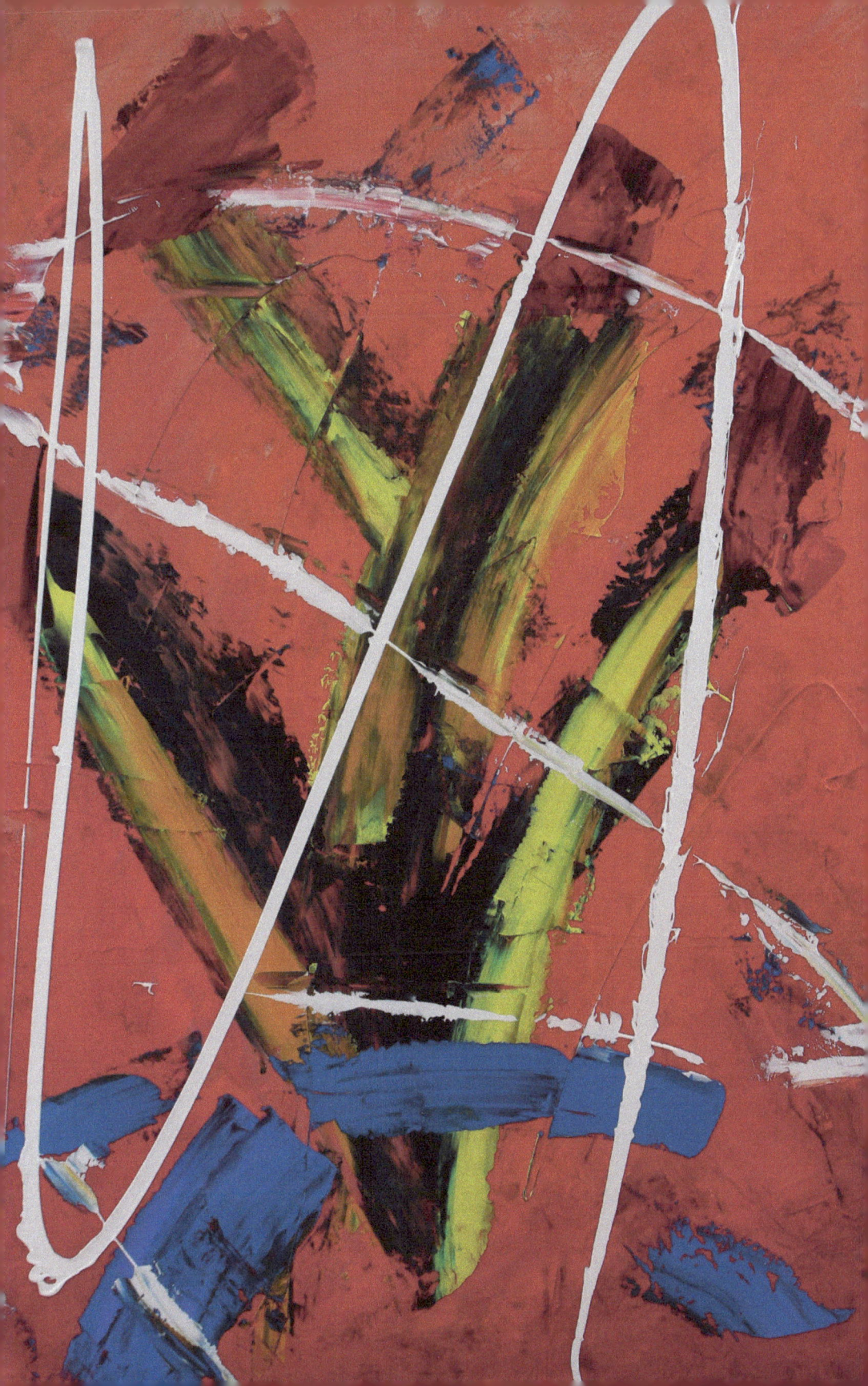

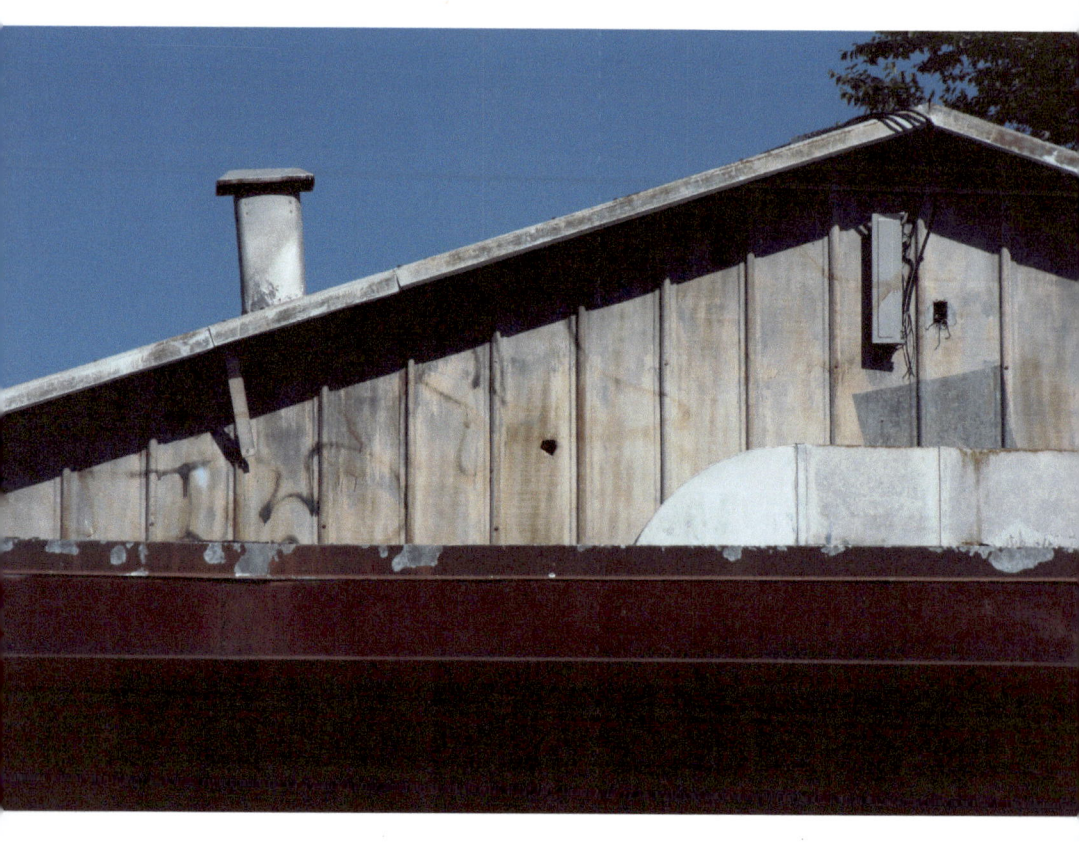

I stared at the newsletter from a church in upper Michigan.

A gift had been given in honor of Joel.

I could easily believe that. Joel was amazing, very fun to be around. But it said the gift had been given "in memoriam." As if Joel were dead.

Joel was 28, tall, athletic, and friendly. He lit up a room whenever he arrived. He liked everybody, laughed easily, and was the kind of person you were glad to know.

He couldn't be gone. He was too full of life.

"In memoriam," it said.

What could the newsletter mean?

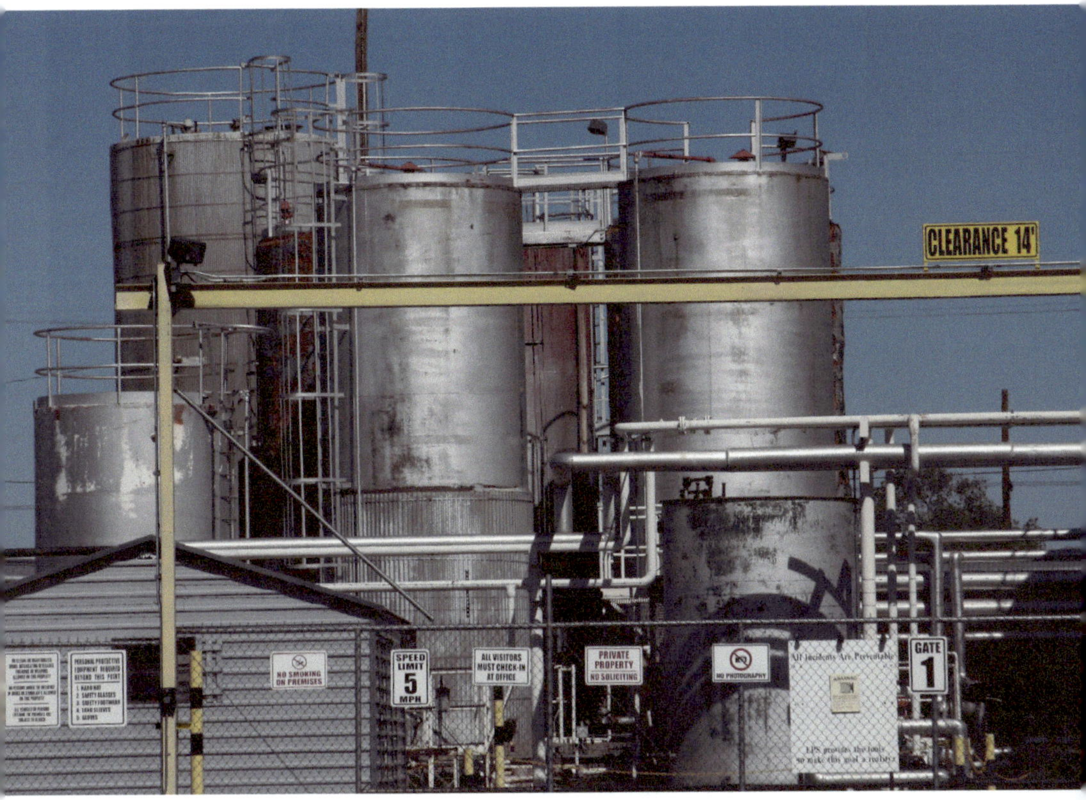

CLEARANCE 14'

NO SMOKING ON PREMISES

PERSONAL PROTECTIVE EQUIPMENT REQUIRED BEYOND THIS POINT
1. HARD HAT
2. SAFETY GLASSES
3. SAFETY FOOTWEAR
4. LONG SLEEVES
5. GLOVES

SPEED LIMIT 5 MPH

ALL VISITORS MUST CHECK-IN AT OFFICE

PRIVATE PROPERTY NO SOLICITING

NO PHOTOGRAPHY

All Accidents Are Preventable

GATE 1

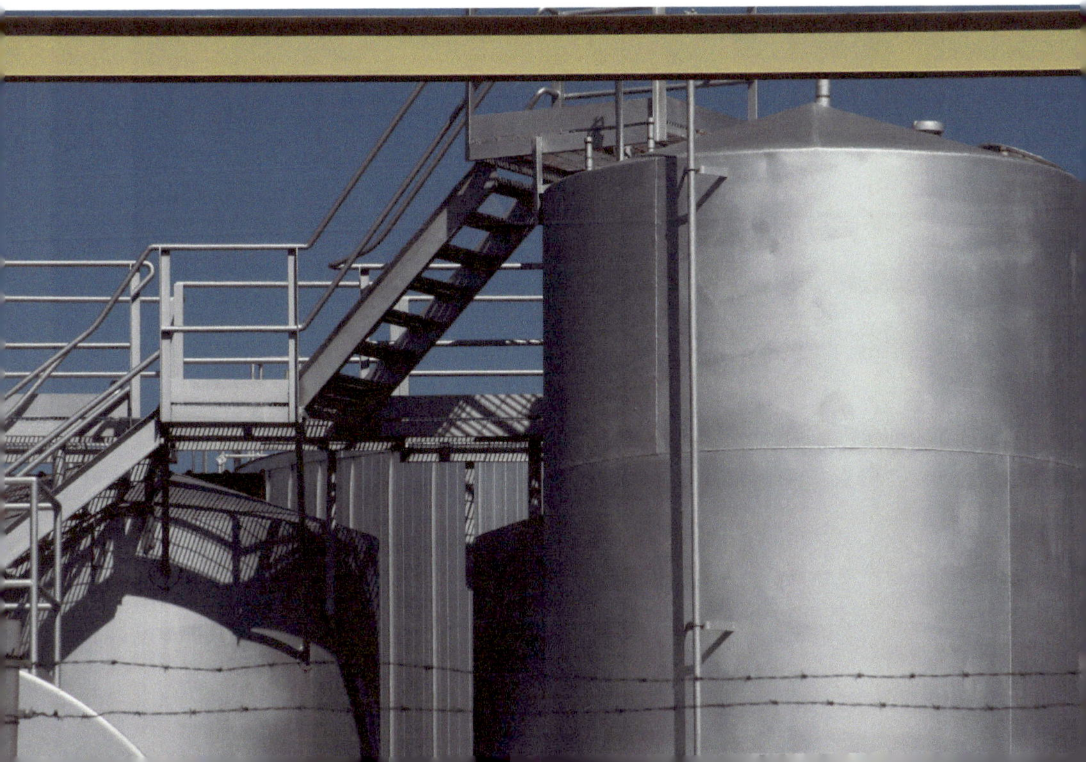

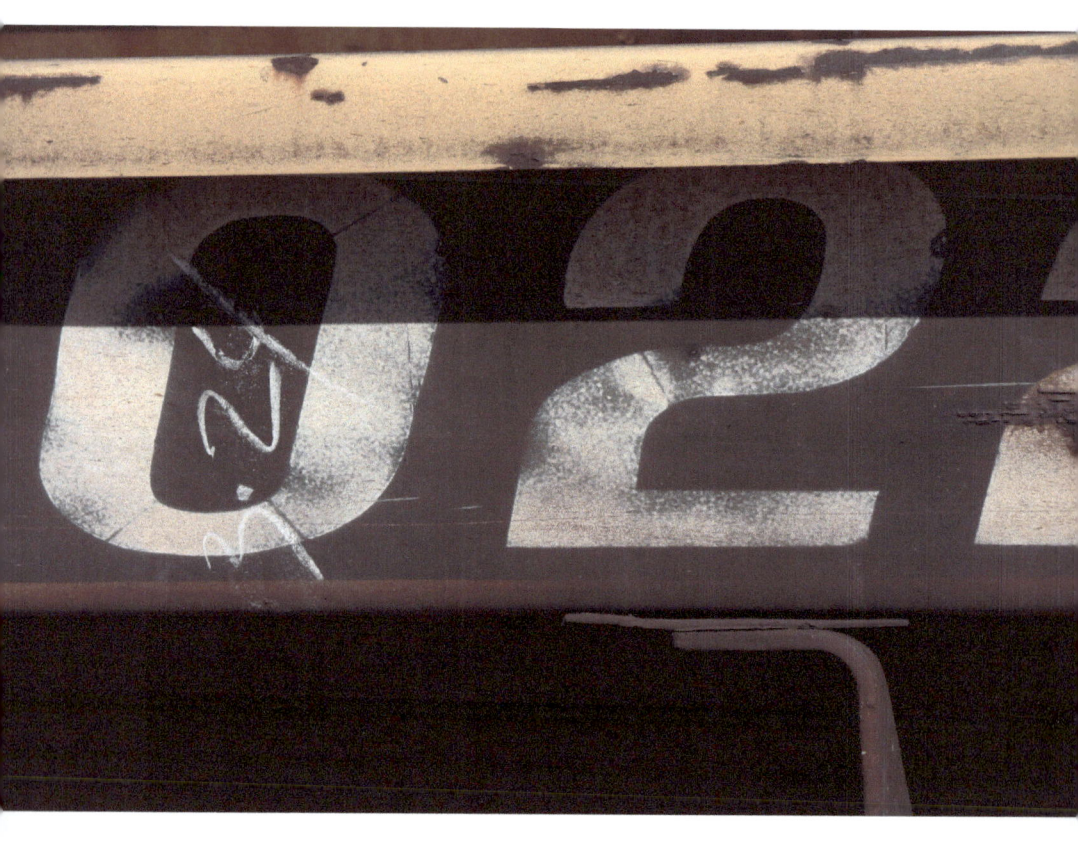

I met Joel in seminary. You couldn't help but thank God that there was someone like Joel who wanted to be a pastor. I smiled every time I thought of him.

Lots of athletes hang out with people who are as skilled as they are. But there aren't many athletes who are good friends not only with the skilled and the swift but also with the clumsy and the slow and the weak. Joel was friendly with everyone.

Joel did his internship at the same congregation where I had been an intern, so I got to read about him from time to time in the church's monthly newsletter. When he graduated, he was hired as a Chicago congregation's pastor for youth and families.

Then one day on a winding highway, Joel's car met another. He was 28.

* * *

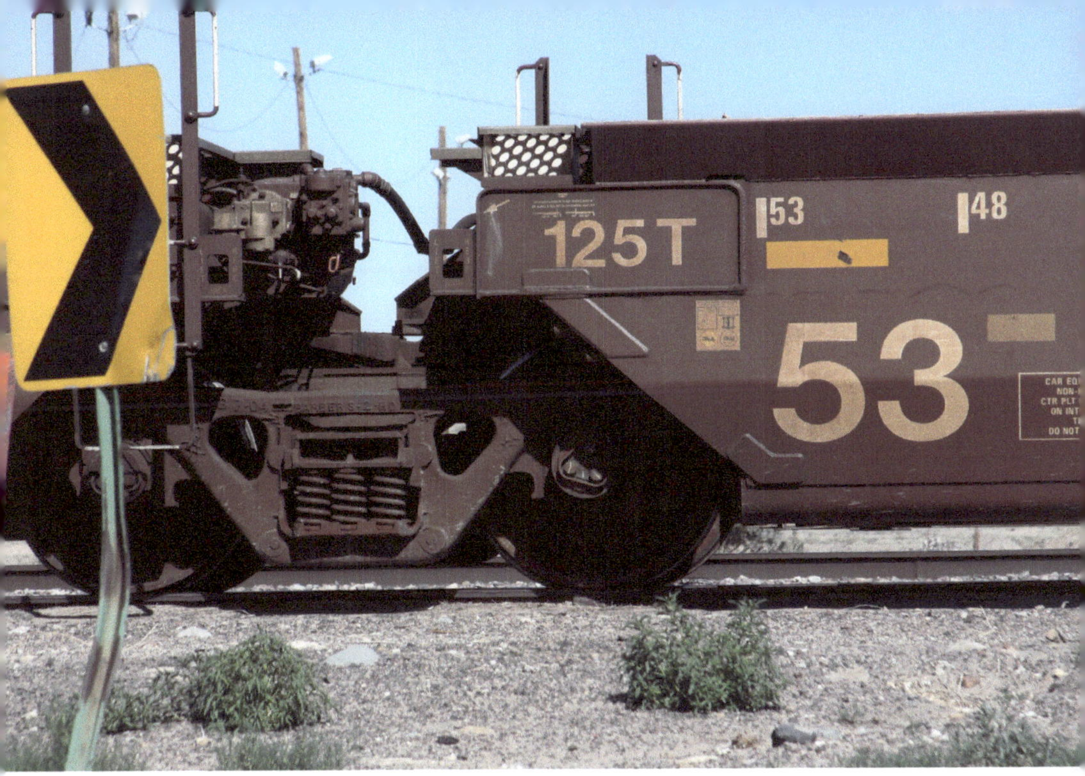

125T 53 48

53

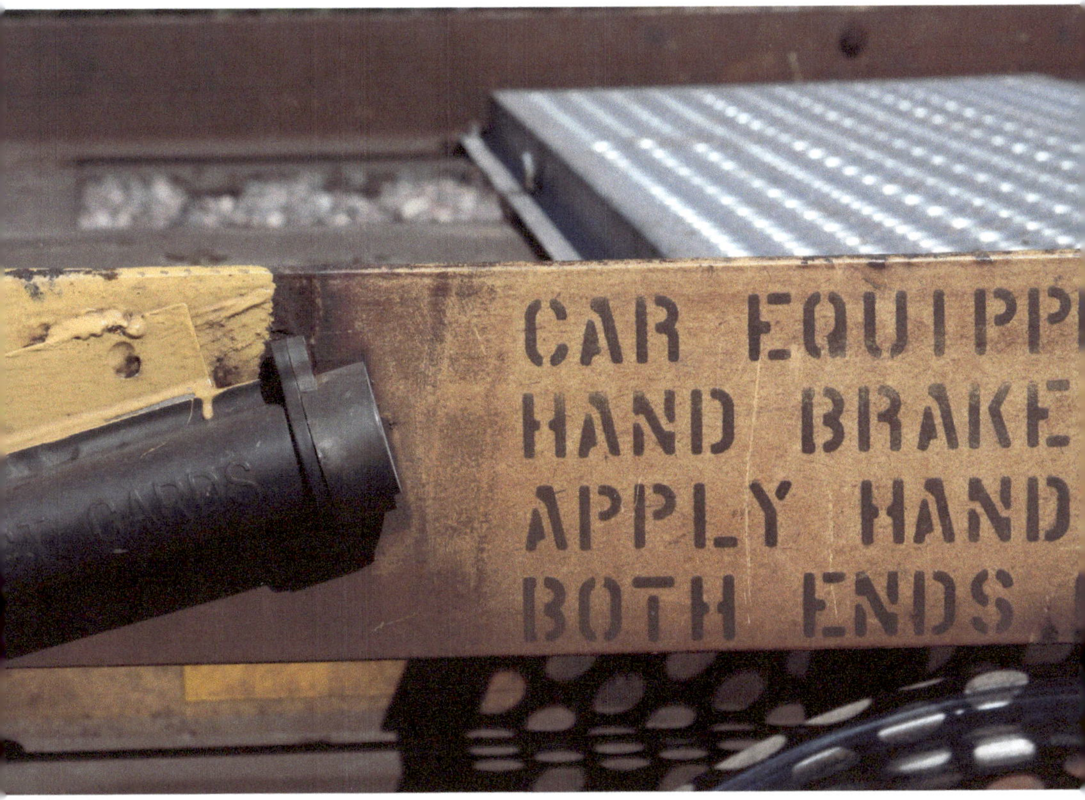

CAR EQ
NON-
CTR PLT
ON INT
TH
DO NOT

CAR EQUIPP
HAND BRAKE
APPLY HAND
BOTH ENDS

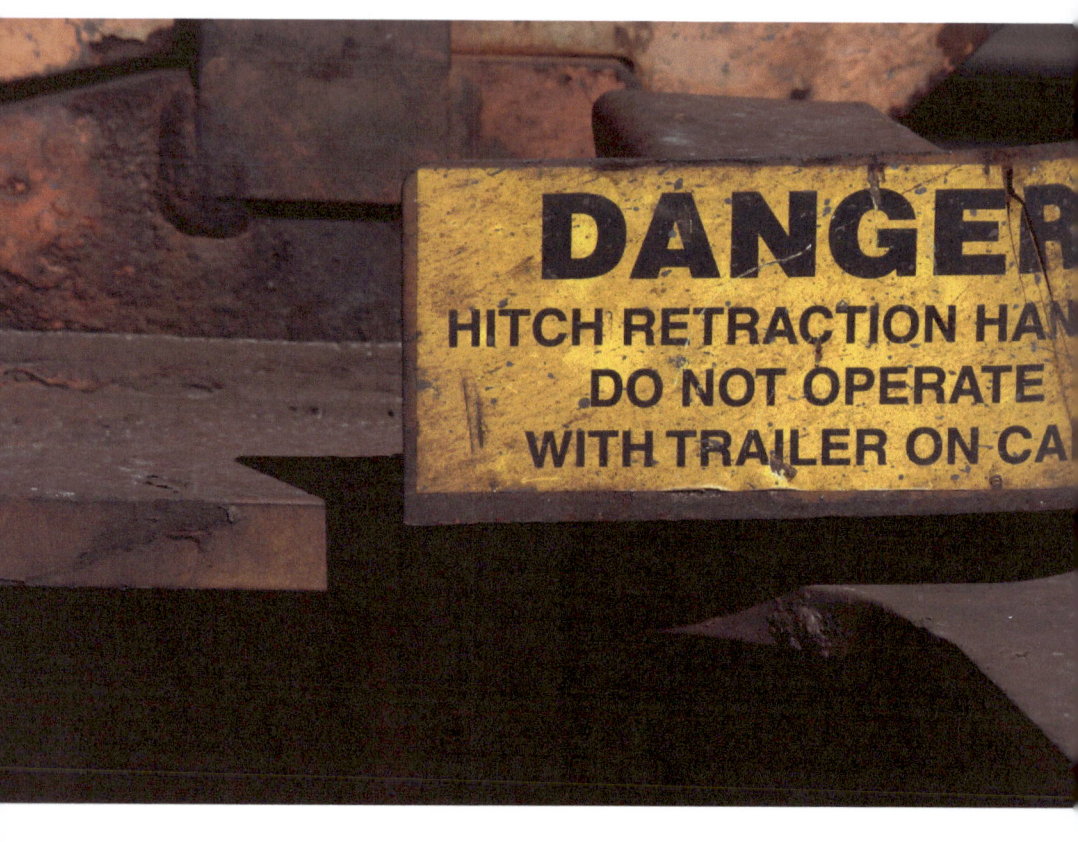

When I found out Joel had died, it was like getting punched.

Joel had been so full of life. So fun to have around. So easy going. So good with people – with kids, with seniors, and everyone in between.

When someone lives a long life, sometimes their last couple years are hard because of health issues. In such cases, even though everyone knows they are better off no longer suffering, it still can be sad to lose them and difficult to let them go.

But when someone young dies, it can be harder to work through. How can they not be getting as many opportunities as other people?

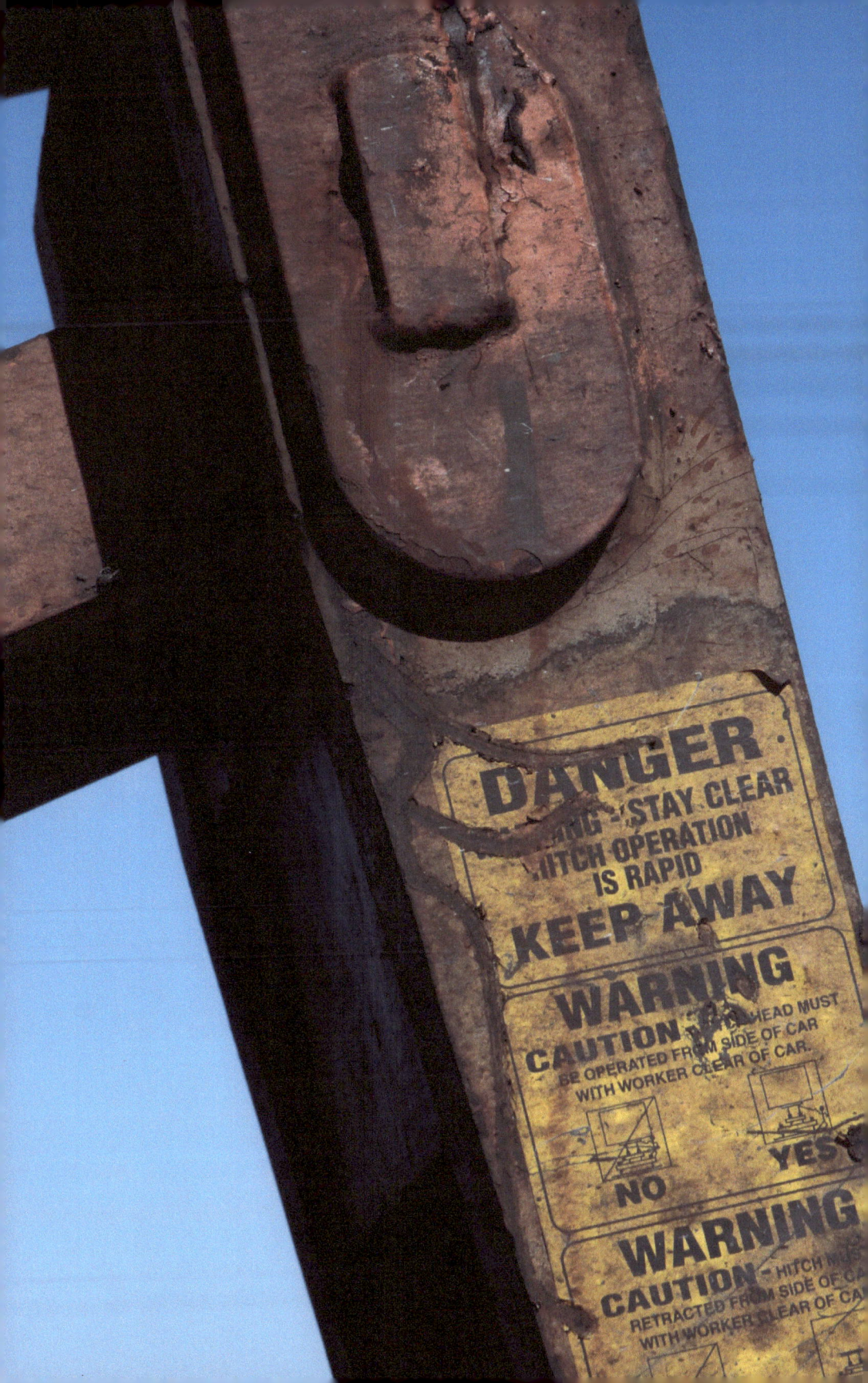

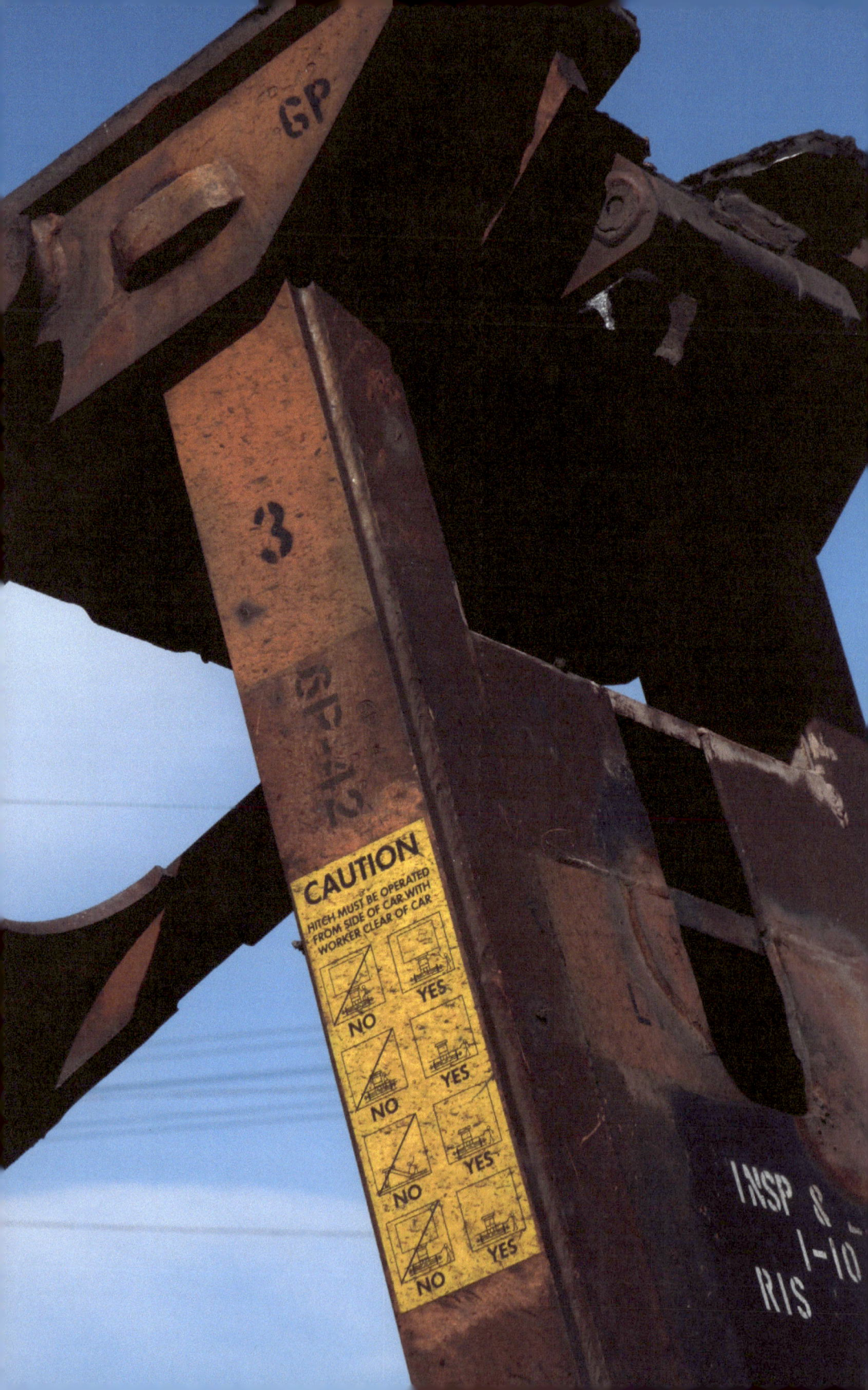

I had moved to a city where no one knew Joel, so I didn't have anyone to talk to who remembered him.

I found it hard to recover.

But a few months later, I thought I was over it.

I just didn't think about it any more.

One Sunday, I visited a church near one of our National Parks. At the start of the service, the pastor told us to greet the people sitting next to us.

I turned to greet my neighbors with a smile. I read their nametag. They had the same last name as Joel.

I burst into tears.

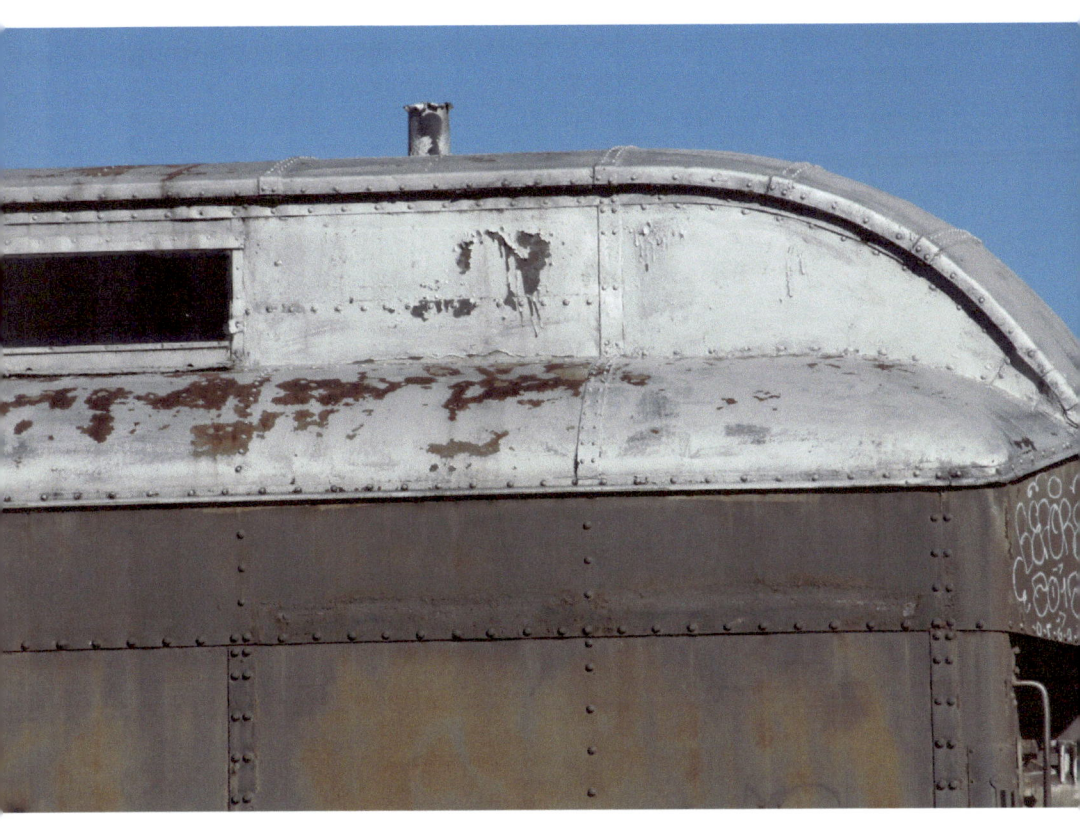

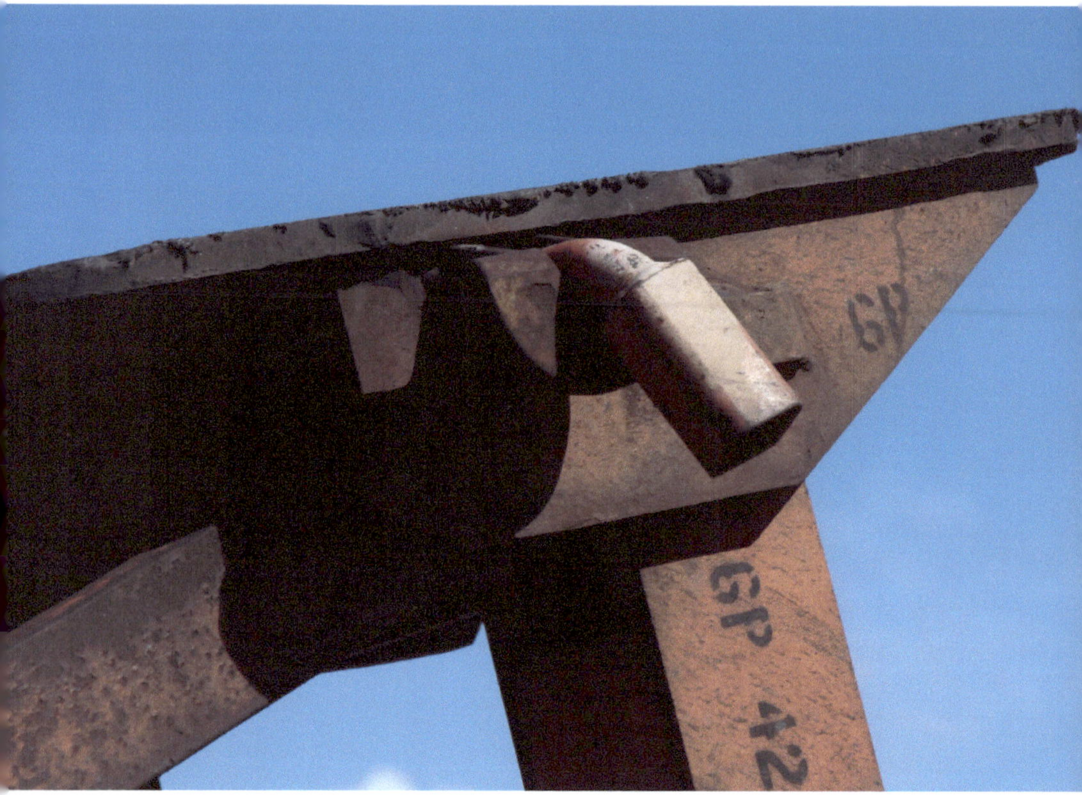
GP
GP 42

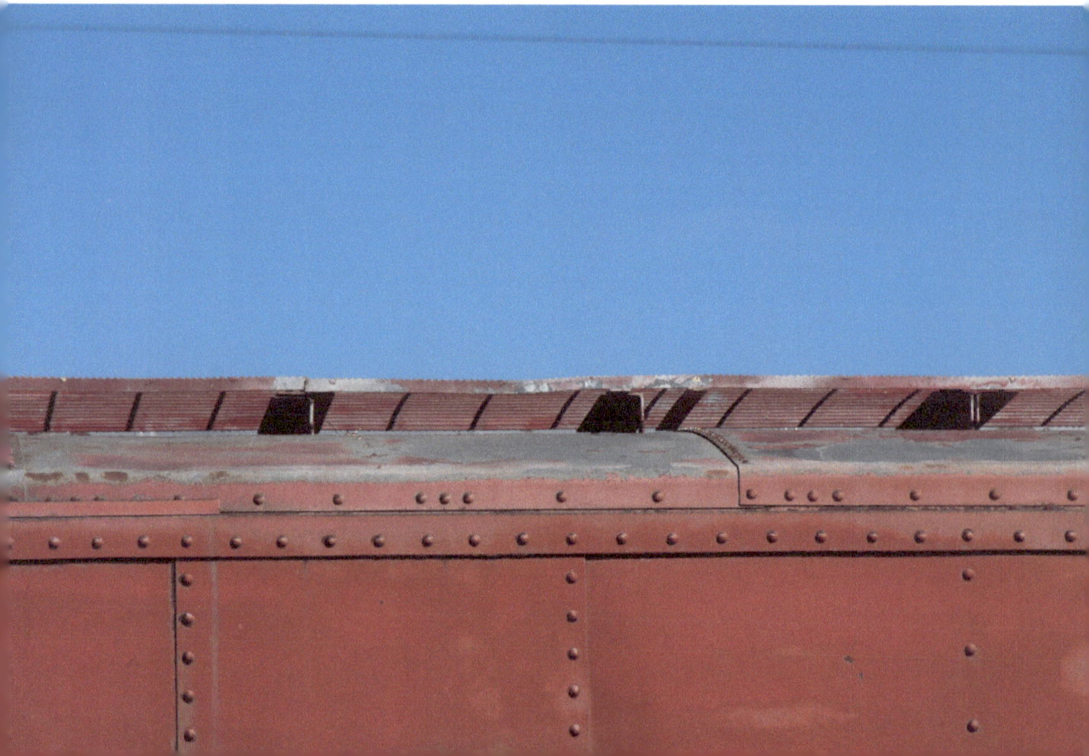

Not some polite, gentle tears welling in the corner of my eyes. No. Instead: Deep, racking, convulsive sobs that engulfed me the second I saw their last name. I went from smiling to inconsolable in an instant.

I couldn't get enough air to tell them what was wrong. I had no ability to be polite. I turned away, stunned and gasping, wrecked, overwhelmed for a long, long time.

That's when I realized I wasn't over it.

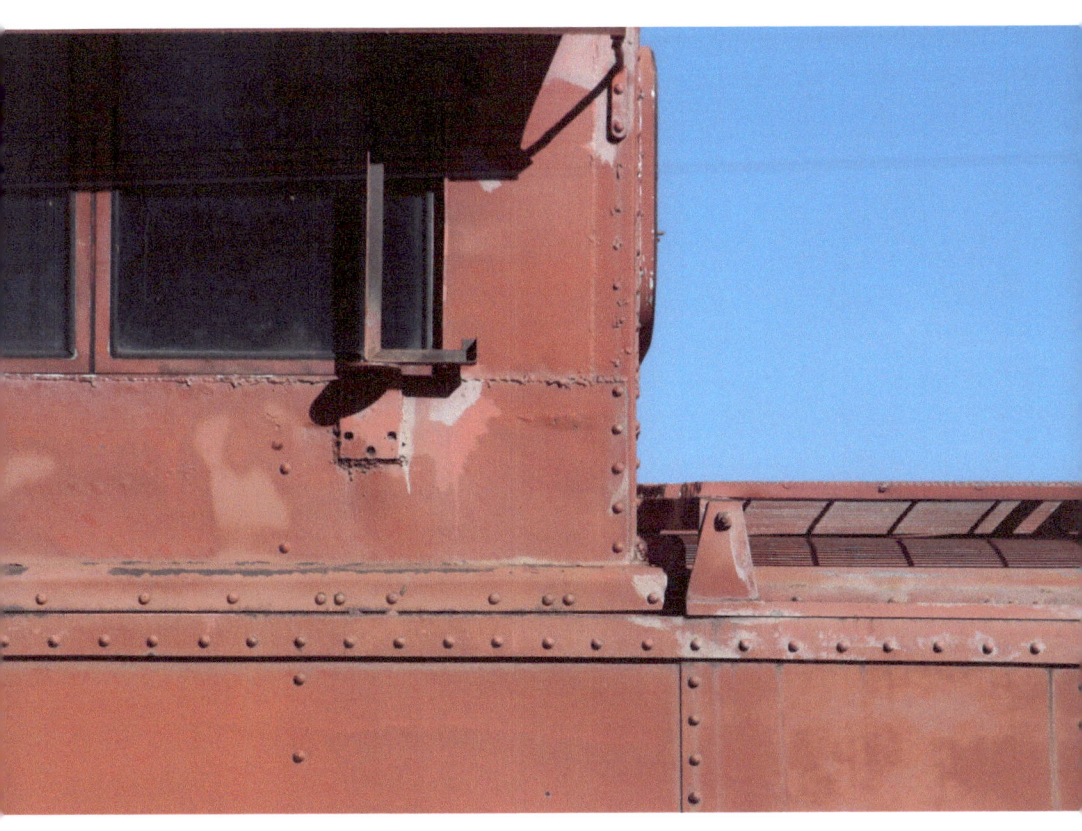

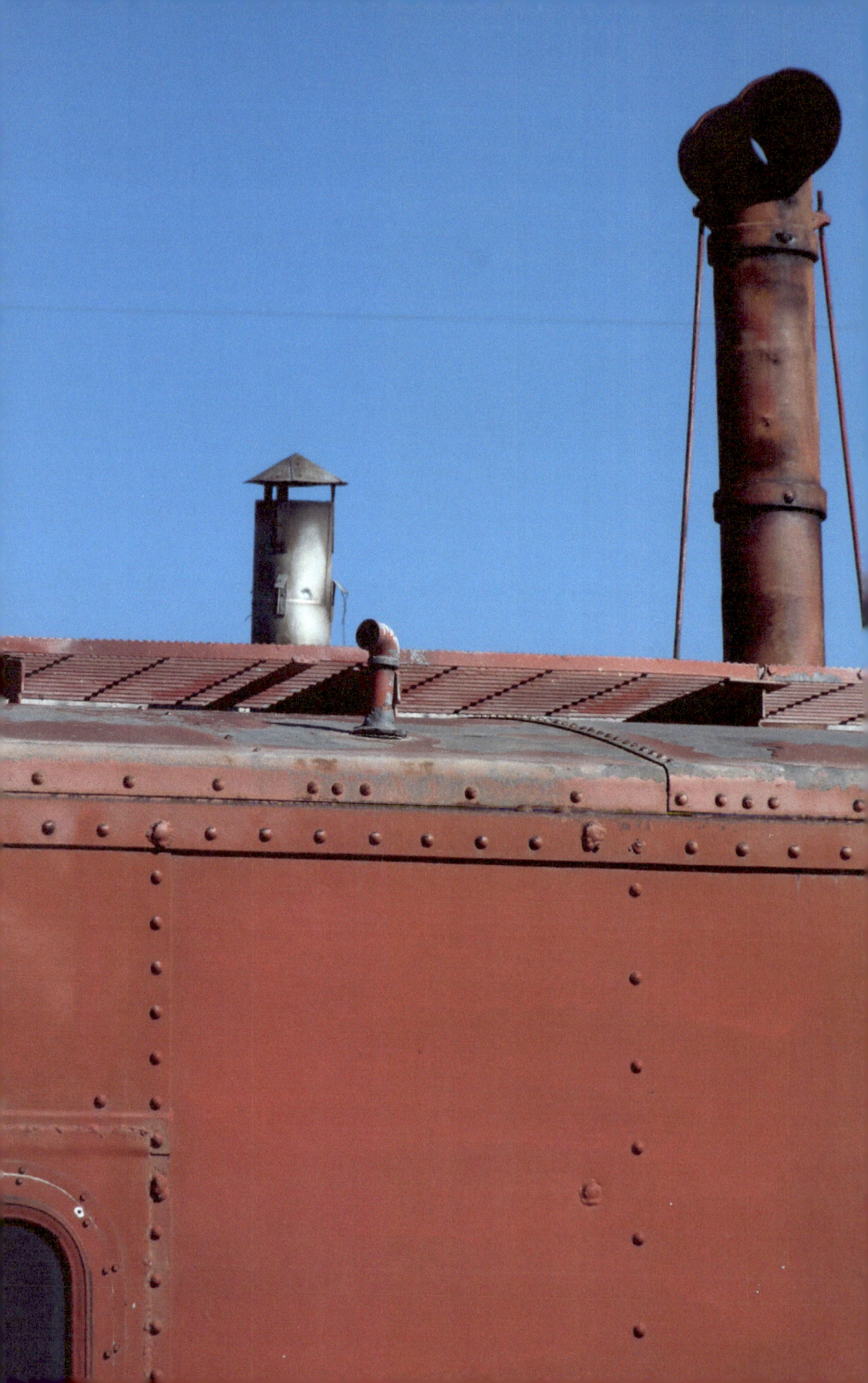

(If you ever meet the couple I sat next to that day, please apologize for me. Sometimes I laugh now when I think how it must have looked, but at the time I couldn't help it. I was caught completely off guard.)

Joel's funeral had been held before I knew he had died. There was no chance for me to go to the service and grieve with friends. But since I so clearly wasn't over Joel's death, I decided to visit his grave.

* * *

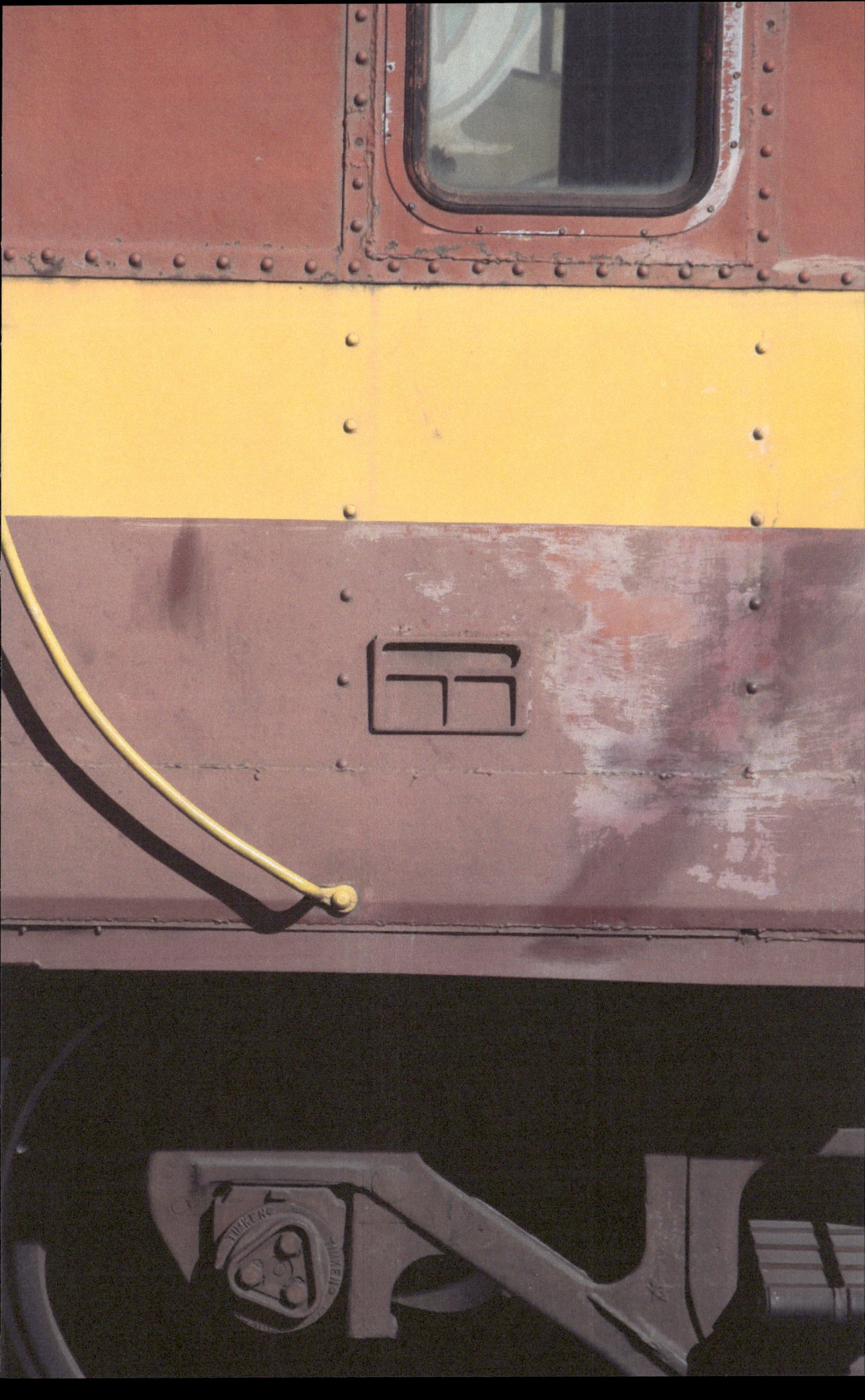

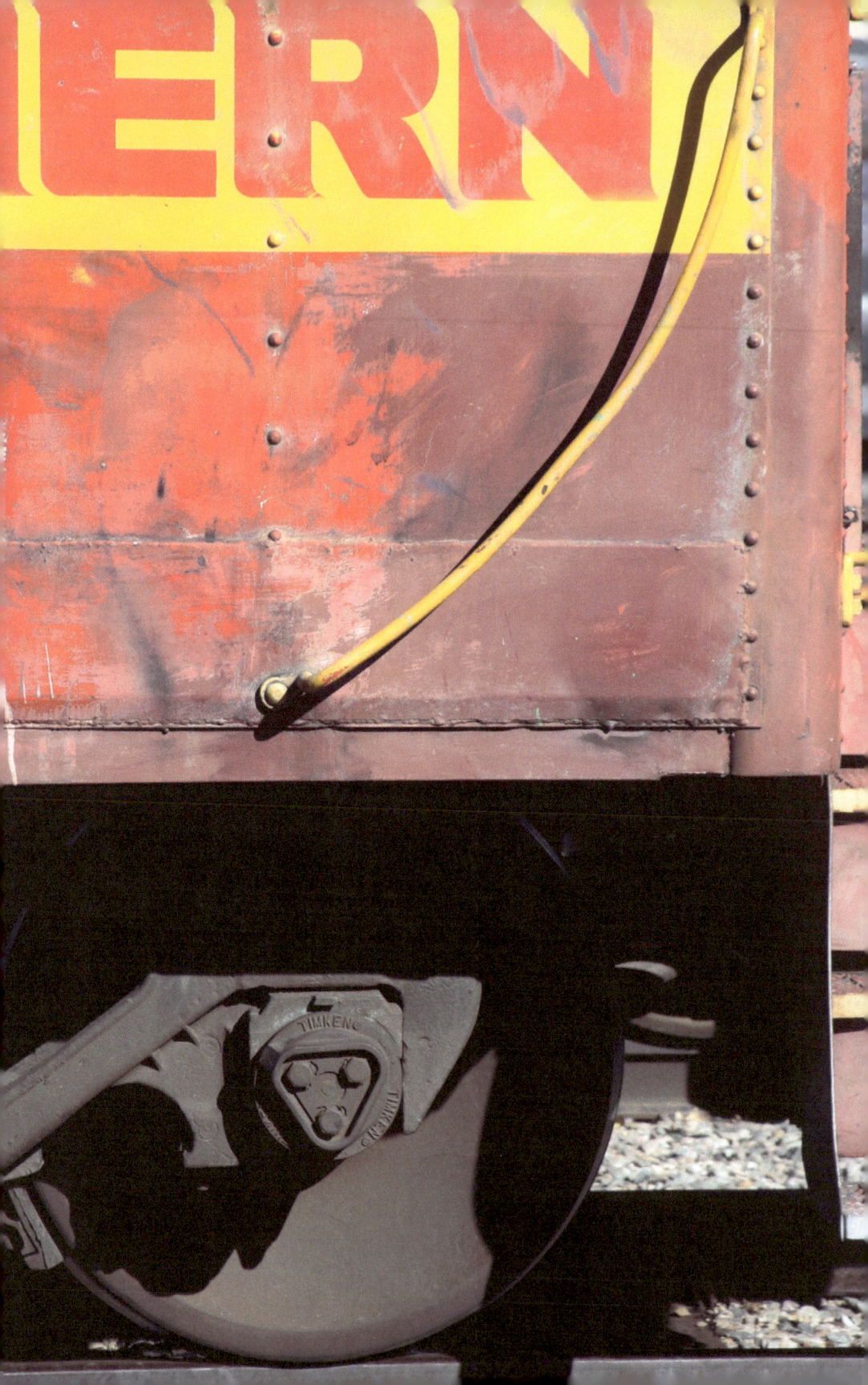

Joel had been buried in a small graveyard at a country church in the Midwest. So on a trip to a nearby city, I rented a car and drove down to the site.

I arrived close to sunset, and went from one marker to the next, dusting off the snow to read the names.

At first I just looked at random, but the sun was going down and I quickly realized I needed to be more systematic. So I started with the first marker in the first row, and went down one row after another, reading the names.

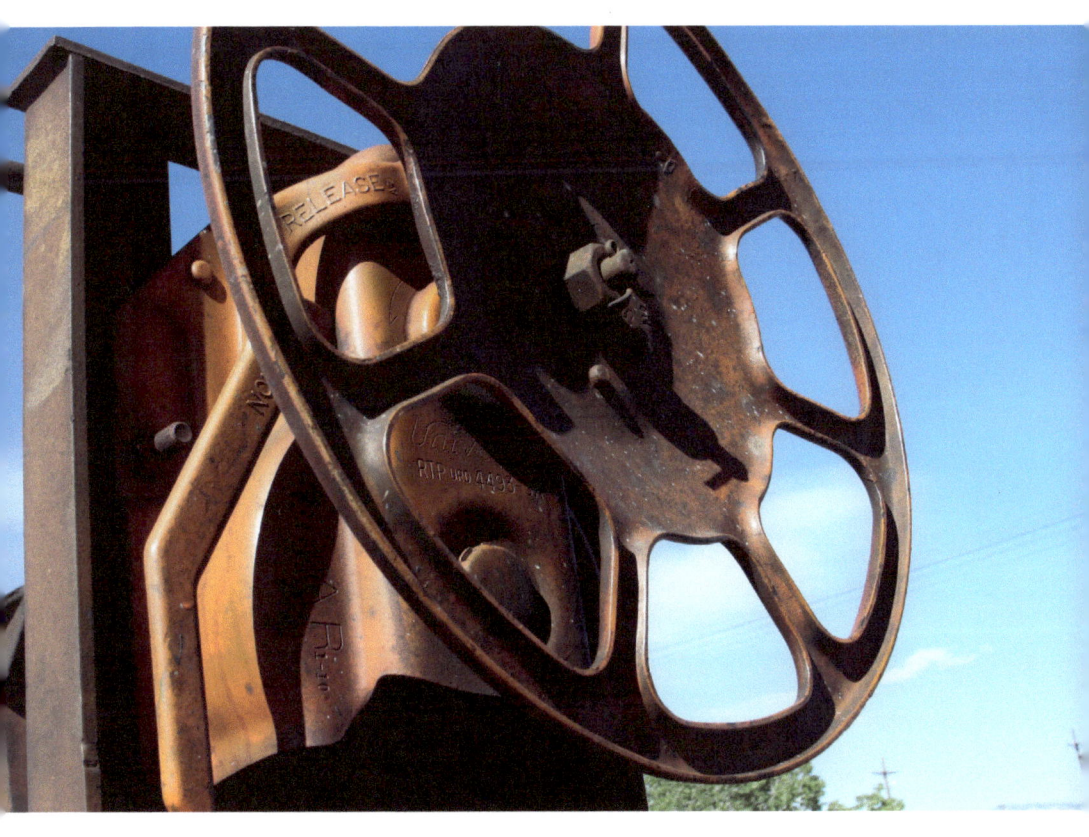

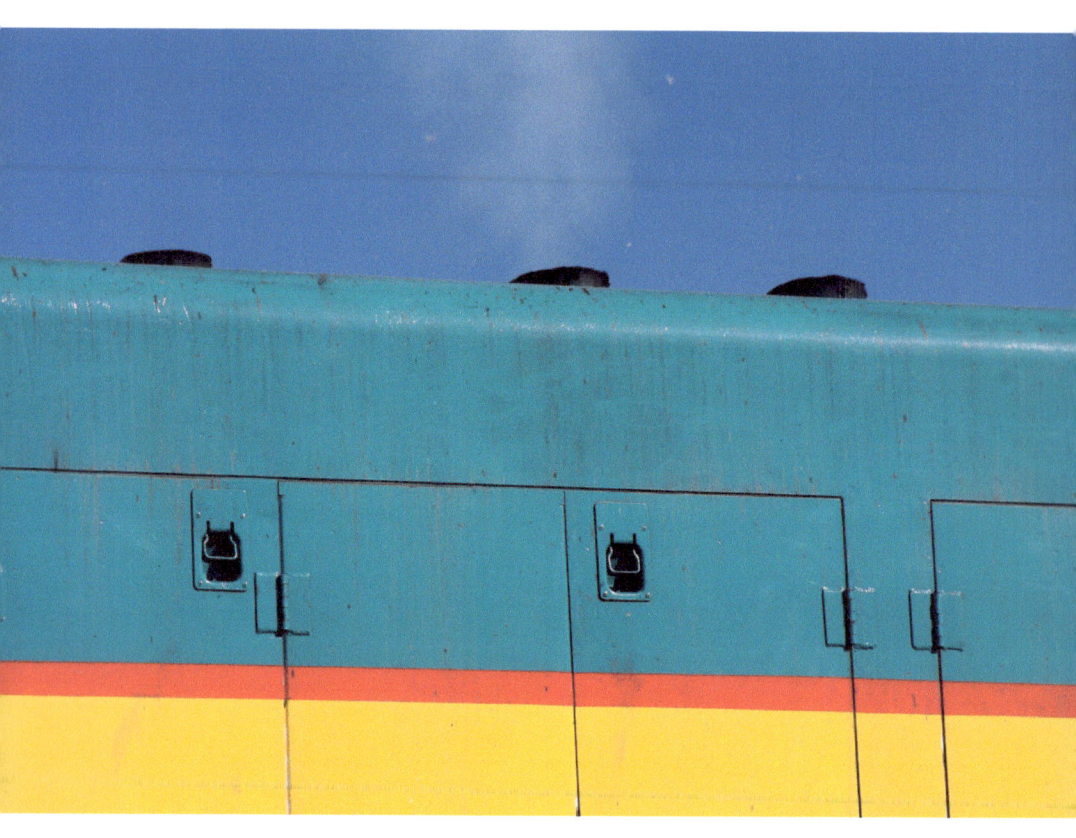

I couldn't find Joel.

***

I didn't know it, but Joel's gravestone hadn't been set up yet. I wasn't going to find Joel's grave, no matter how hard I searched. But I learned that only later.

I continued to look at one marker after another as the sun set and the light faded. Soon it would be too dark to see.

"God," I said. "I can't find Joel's grave."

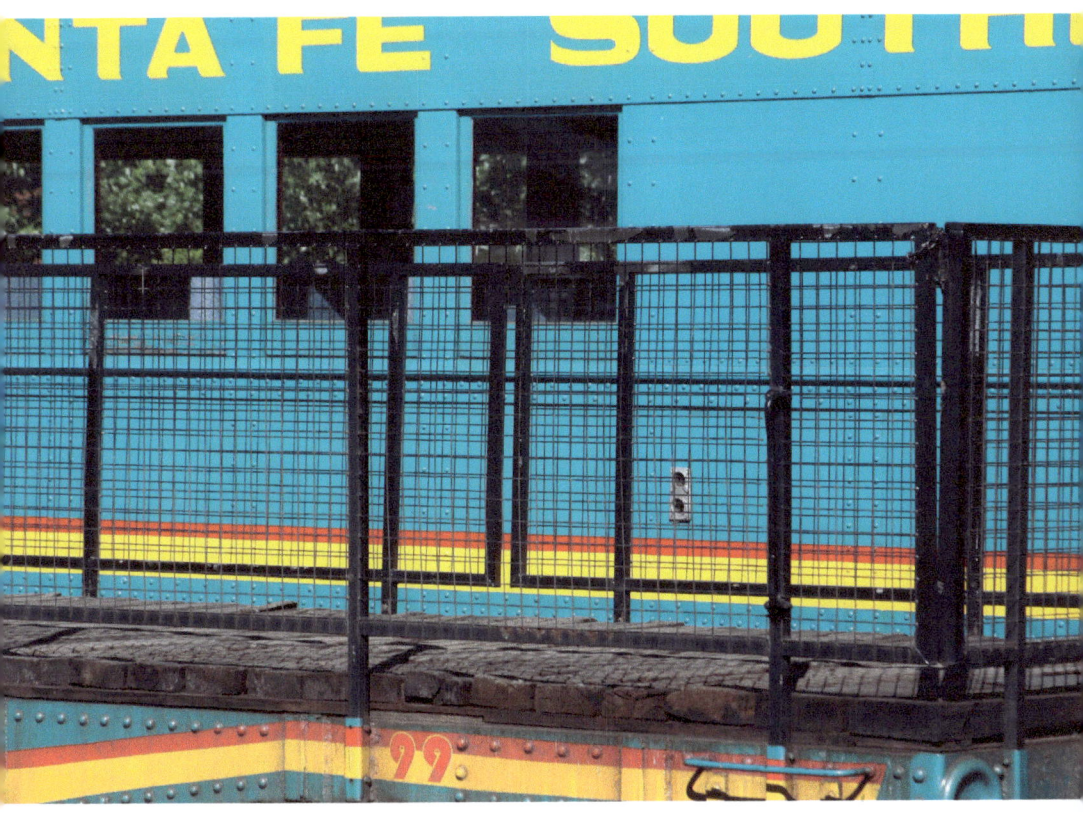

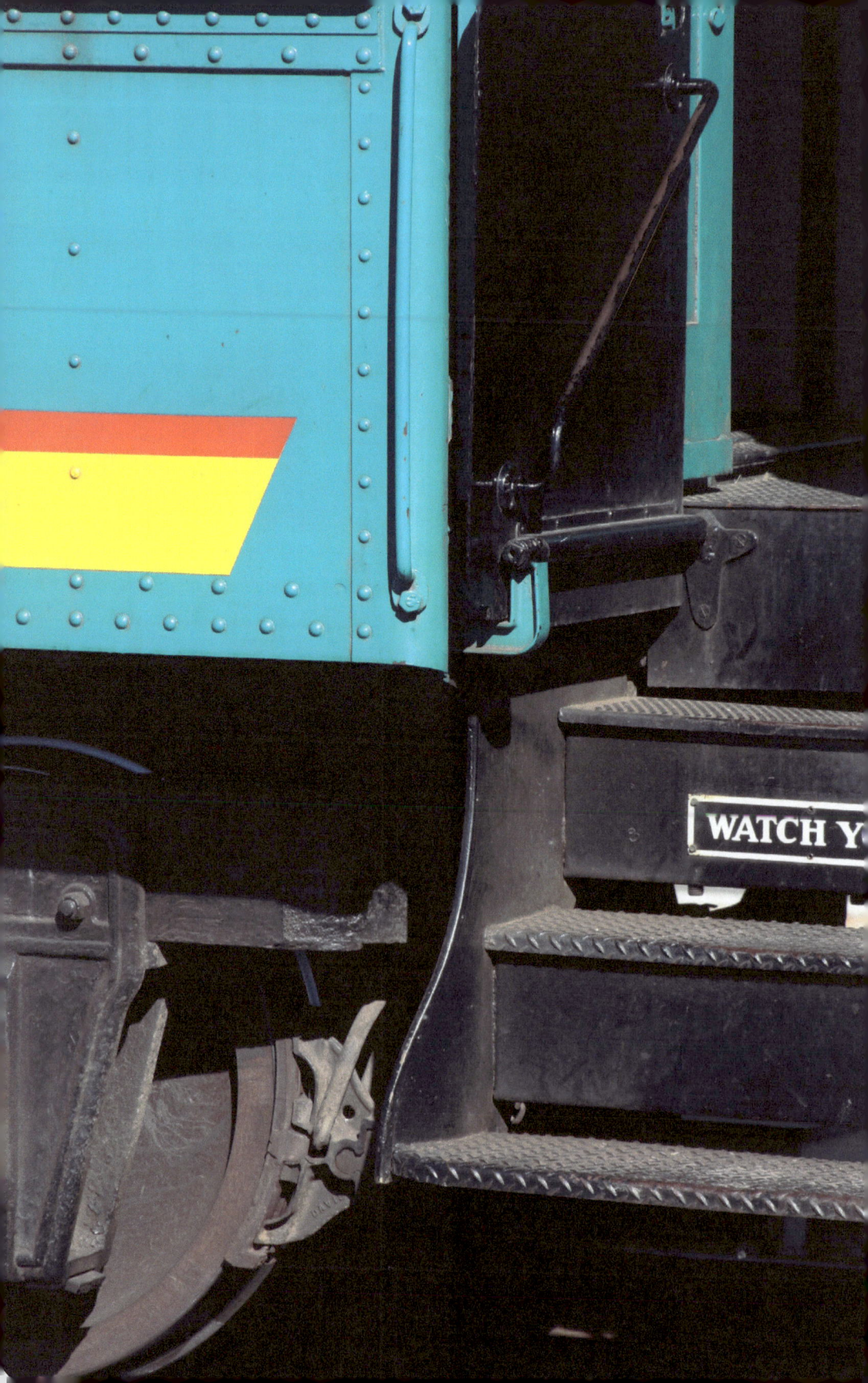

You may not ask God for help when you can't find something, but I recommend it. I usually don't ask until after I've looked quite a while on my own. But when I'm stuck, I talk to God about it. And over the years I've found that God never loses track of my keys or whatever else I'm searching for. Almost always I find what I'm looking for within a minute of asking for help.

"God, I can't find Joel."

Usually, when I make a request like this, I have a faint sense of where to look. But this time, something unusual happened. Instead of sensing where I could find Joel's grave marker, a phrase from the Bible suddenly came to mind.

"Why do you look for the living among the dead?"

* * *

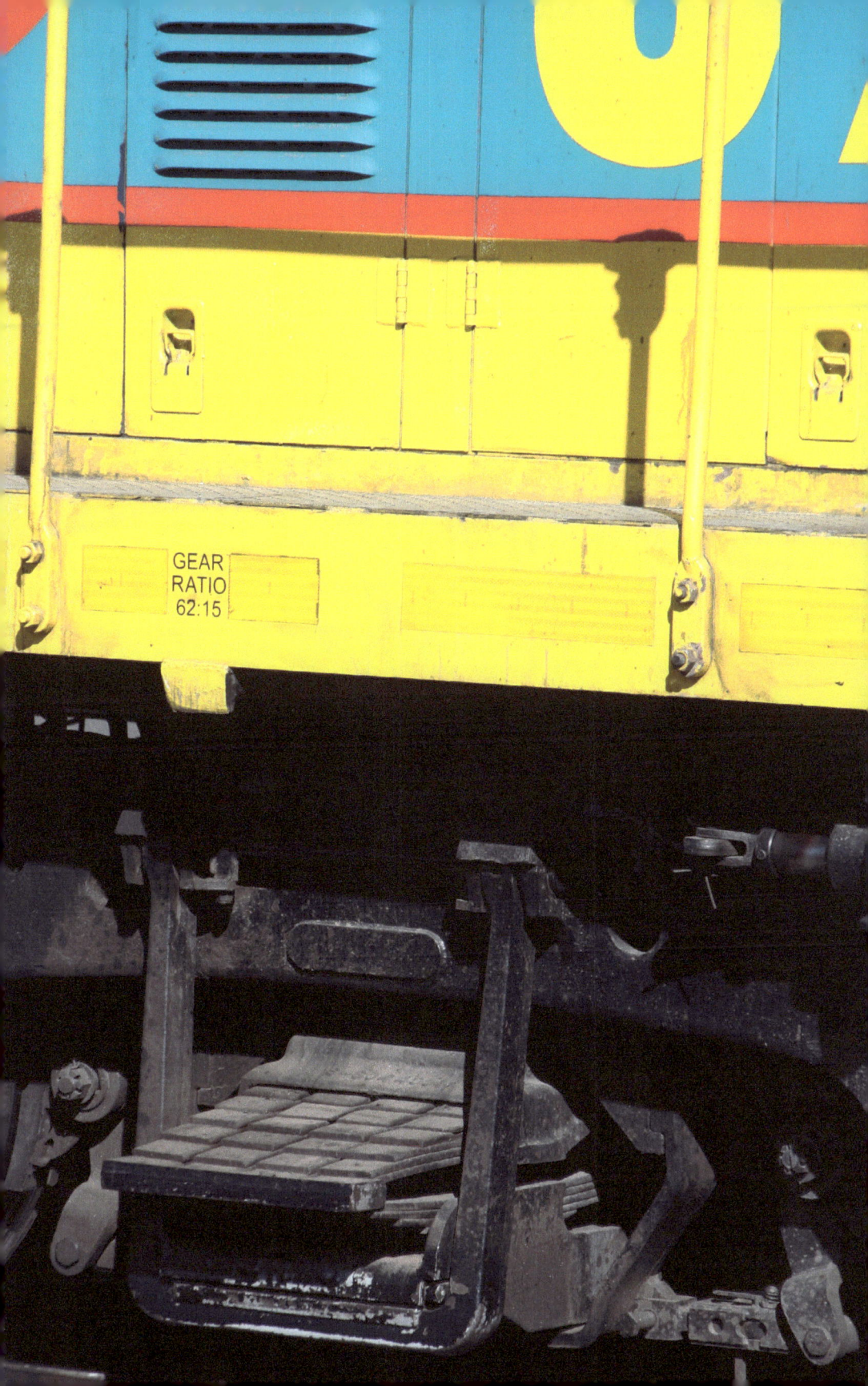

GEAR
RATIO
62:15

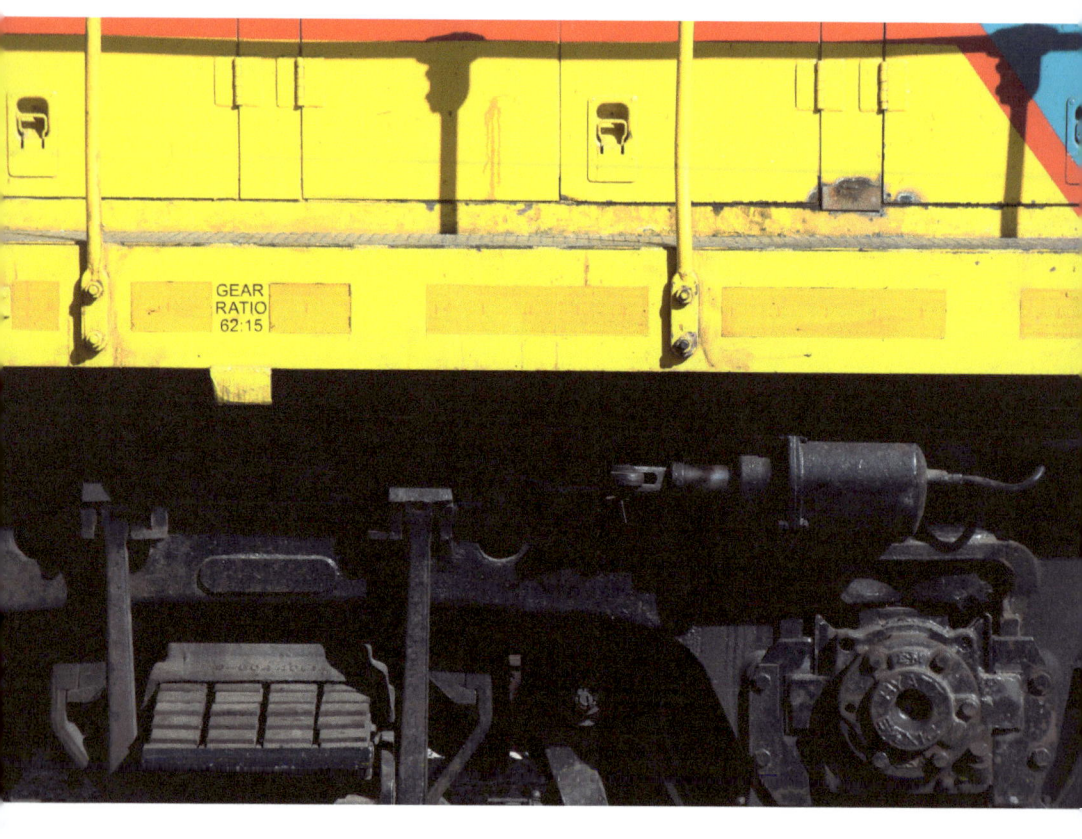

GEAR
RATIO
62:15

Here's a little background:

The Bible says Jesus died on the cross on a Friday. In those days, travel was prohibited on Saturday, so his friends were not able to visit his grave the day after his death. But early Sunday morning, several women hurried to Jesus' tomb. To their surprise, they found it empty. Jesus' body was not there.

When they paused at the scene, wondering what had happened, they were met by two men in dazzling clothes who asked, "Why do you look for the living among the dead?"

The men told them that Jesus had been raised, and he wasn't there.

If you want, you can read this story in the Bible, in Luke 24:1-8.

* * *

Unable to find Joel's gravesite, this same phrase came to my mind.

"Why do you look for the living among the dead?"

I stopped walking through the snow and paused in wonder.

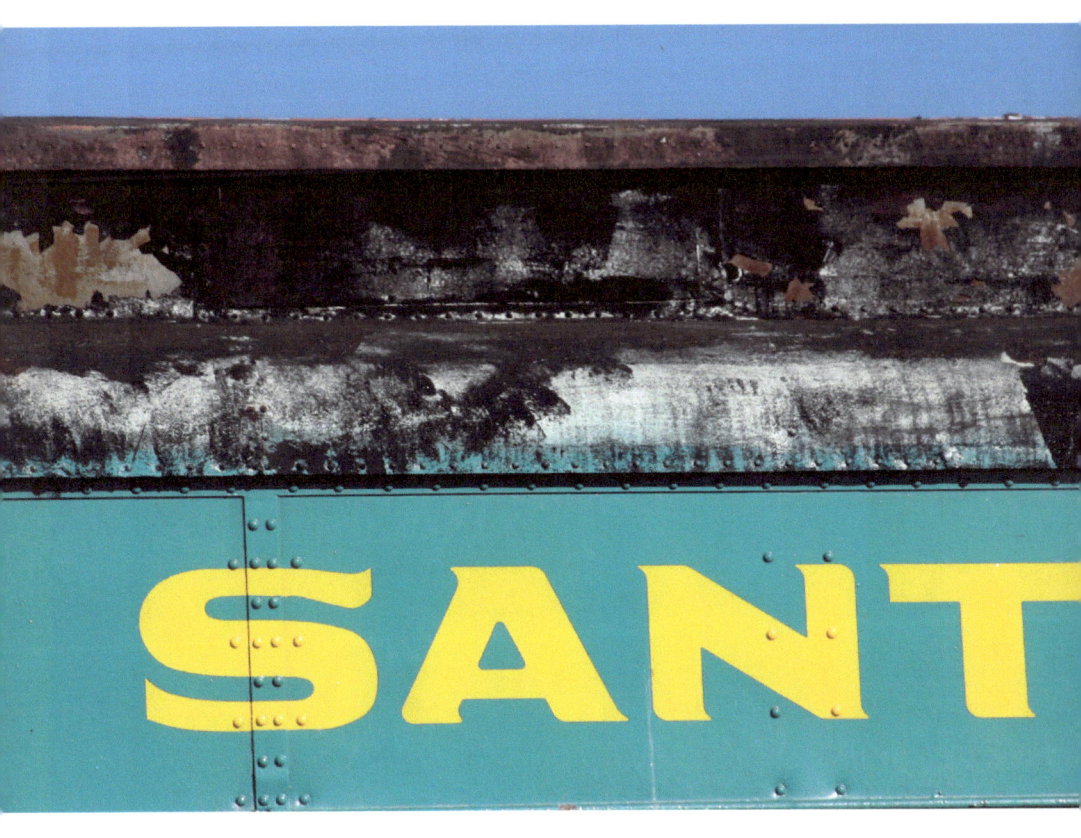

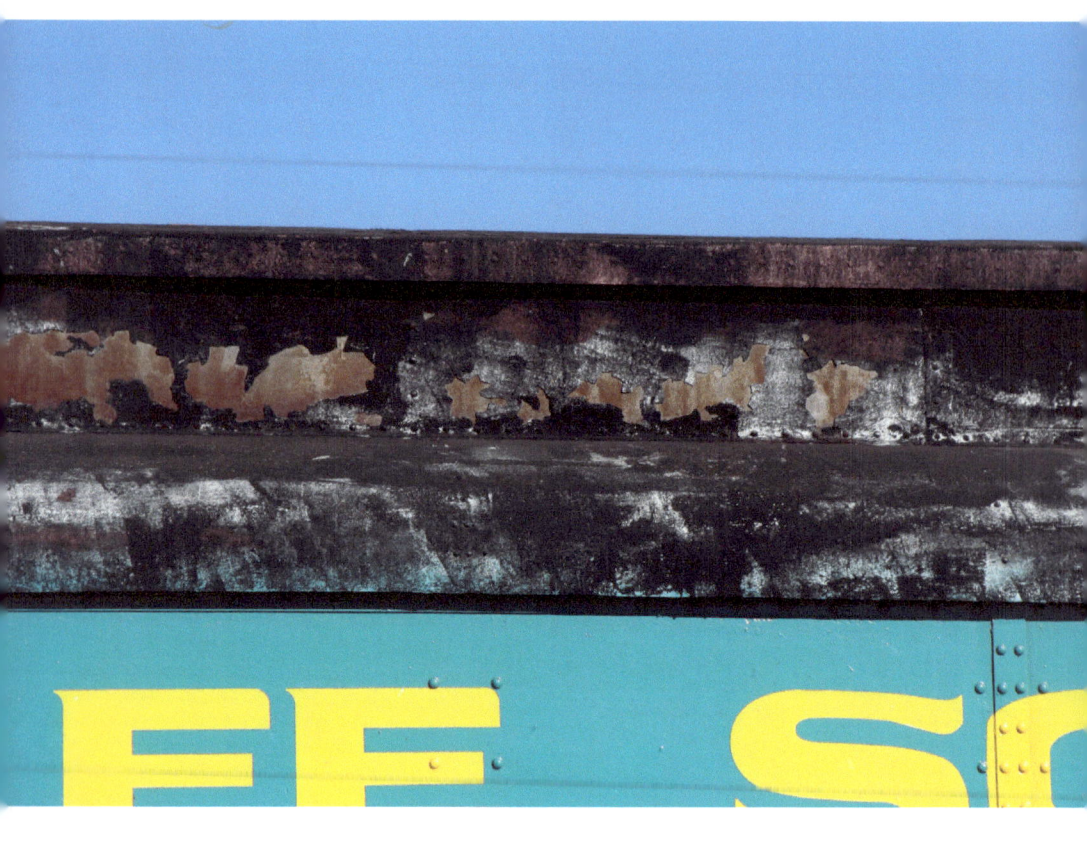

Joel wasn't there. At least not the part of Joel that I missed.

I suddenly realized that I didn't miss Joel's corpse.

I missed his laughter and his smile, the way he loved everyone he met, the energy he brought to a conversation, the joy he deposited in a room. I missed his spirit. And that wasn't buried in this small snow-covered group of graves by a country church.

* * *

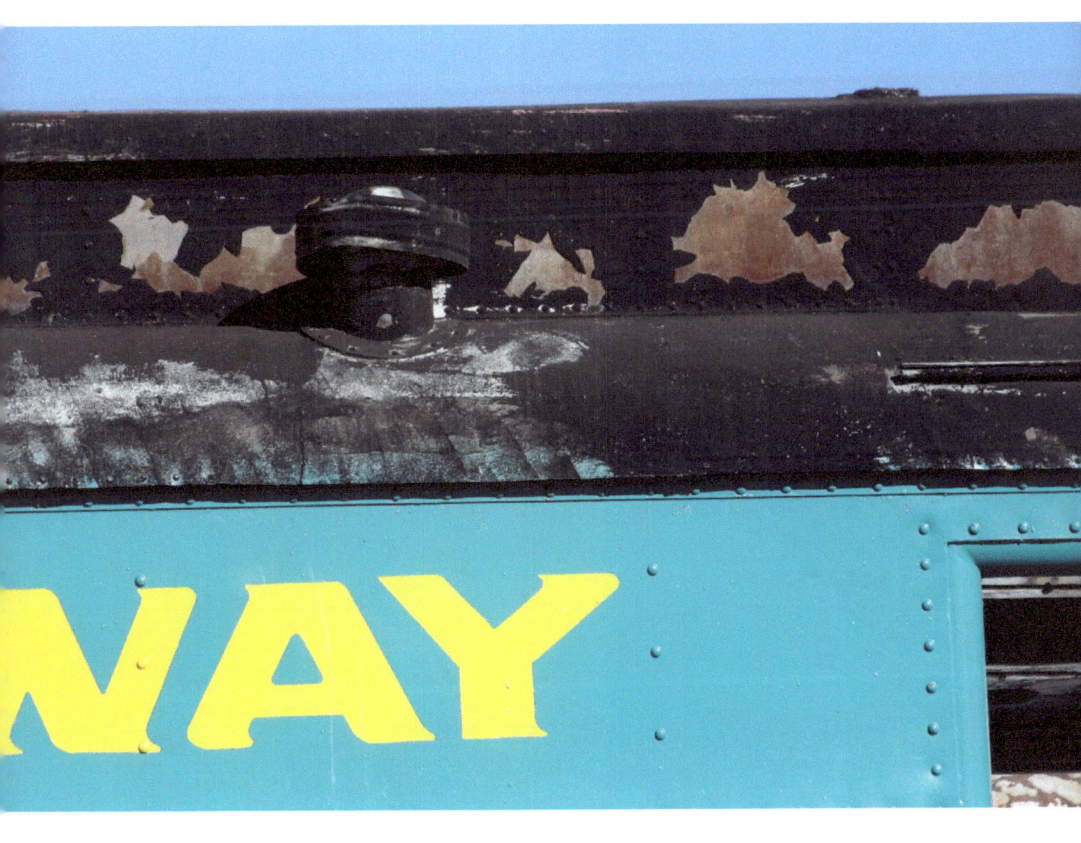

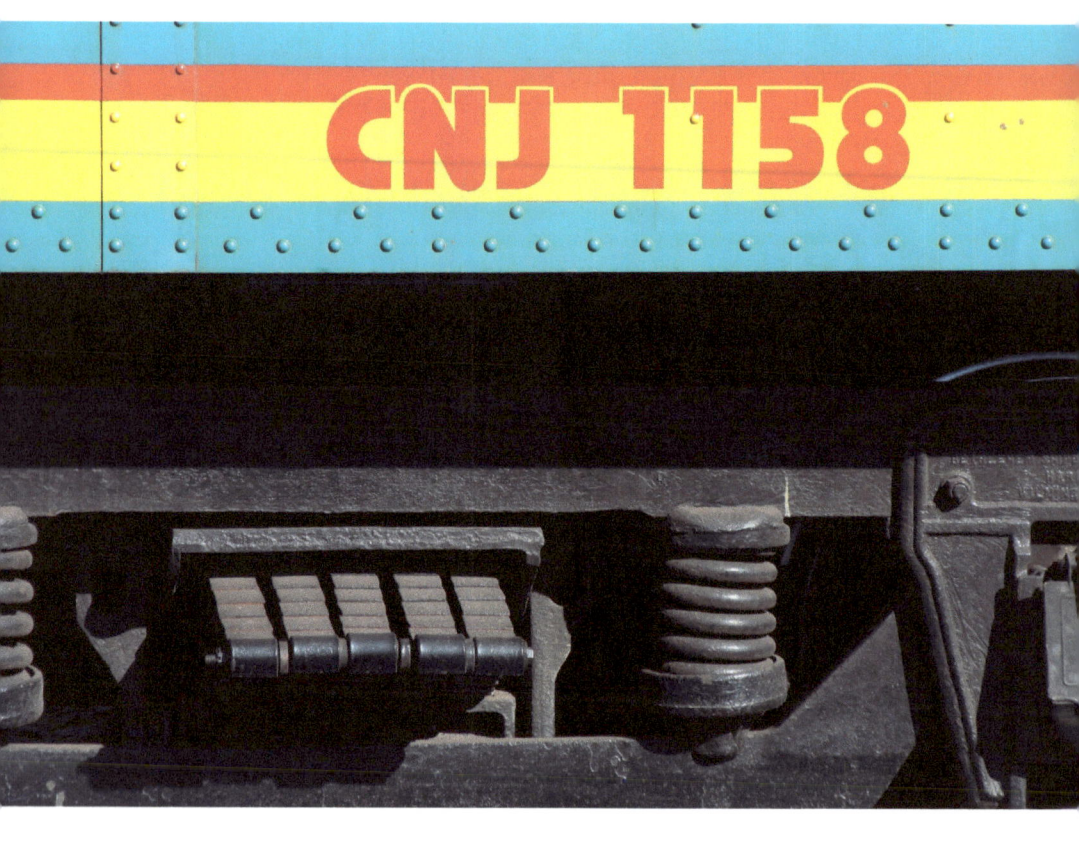

It may be that from time to time you, also, will miss someone who made you smile. If they have died, I think it's okay to go to their grave to remember them. But they're not there – not the part of them that you miss.

There's no sense looking for the living among the dead.

At least that's what I learned when I was finding Joel.

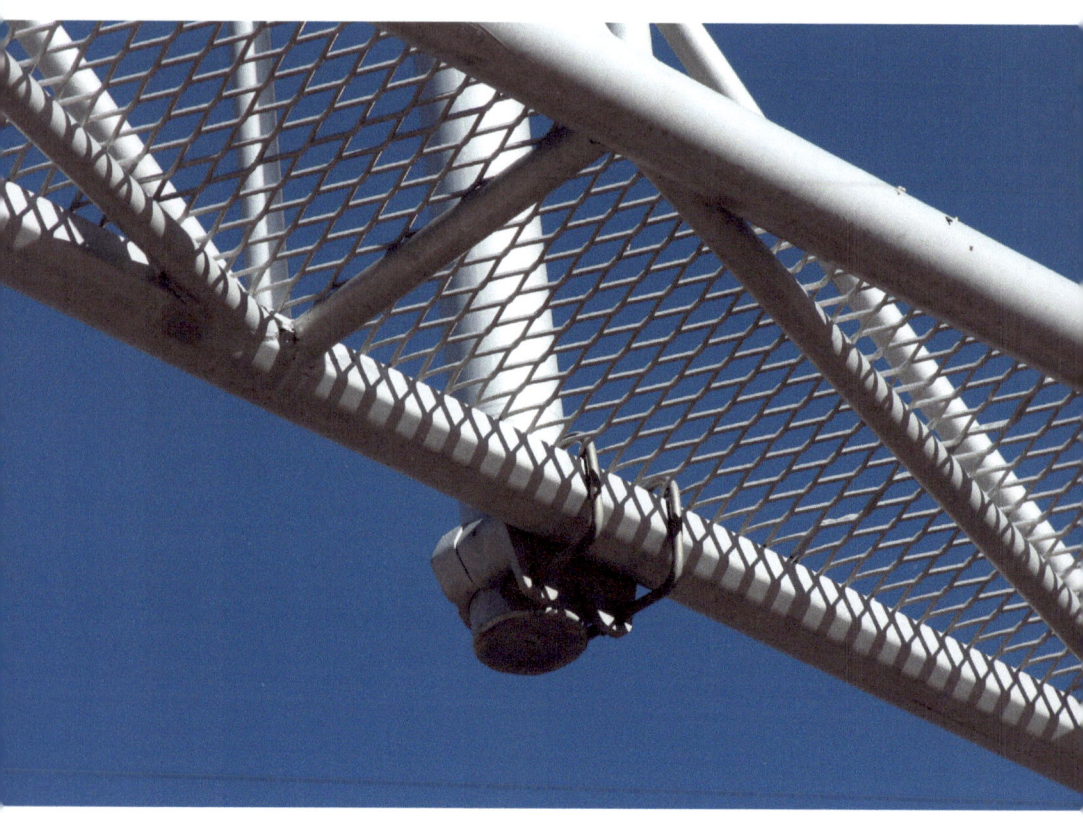

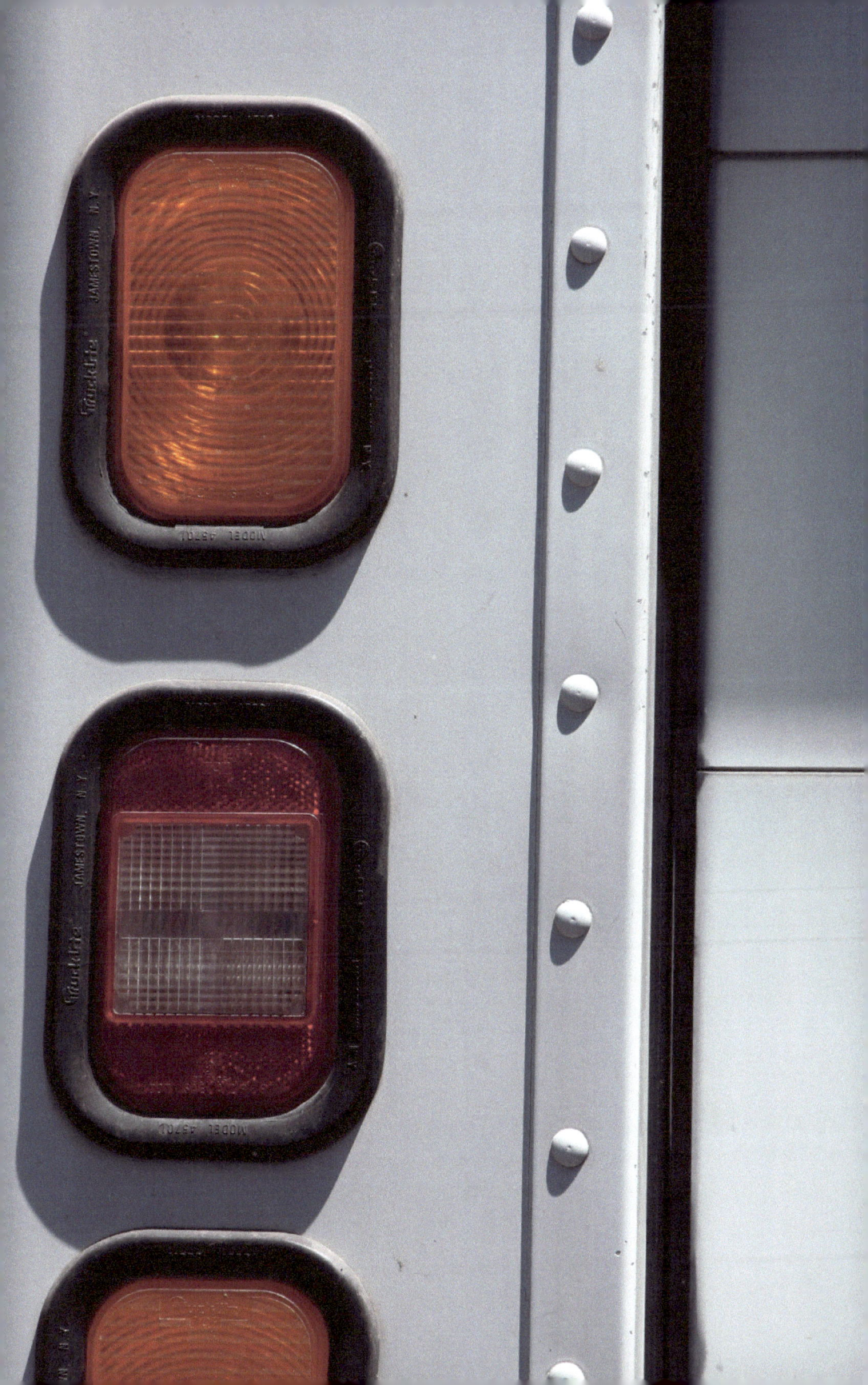

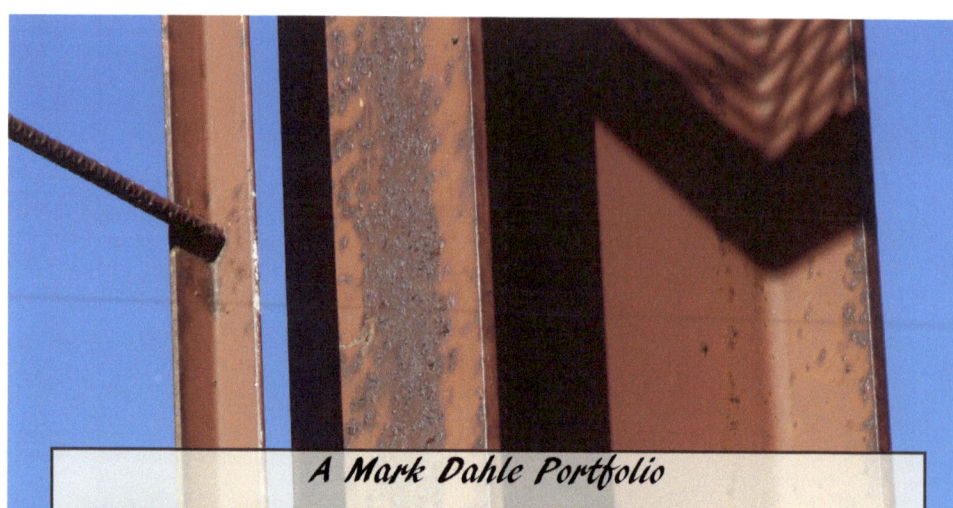

A Mark Dahle Portfolio

Race Day

This Mark Dahle Portfolio includes a beautiful painting, twenty-five outstanding industrial photographs from Minneapolis, and a story about a man going on a race (but picking up things to carry from the people around him).

What (if it's not too impolite to ask), what are *you* carrying?

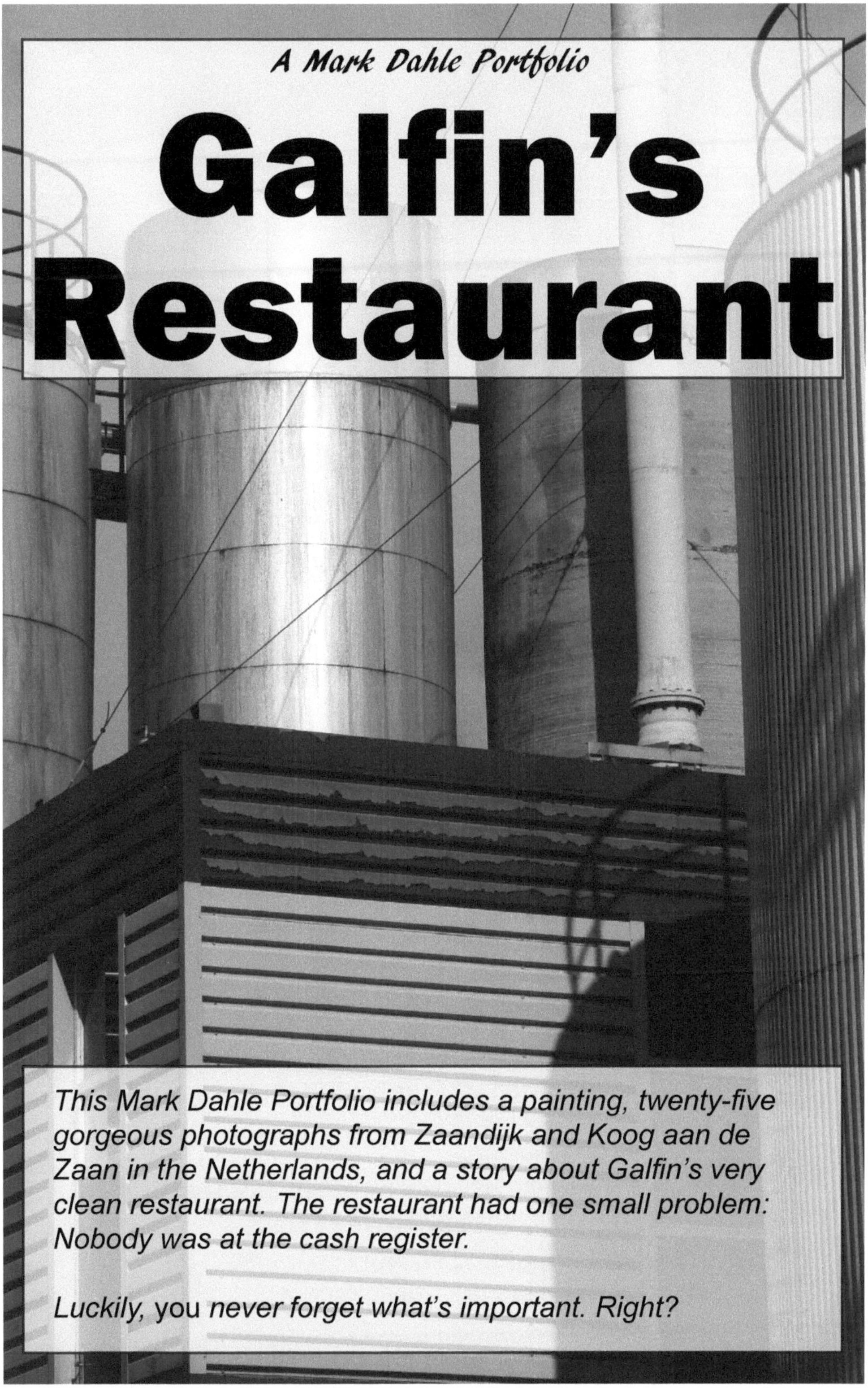

Galfin's Restaurant

This Mark Dahle Portfolio includes a painting, twenty-five gorgeous photographs from Zaandijk and Koog aan de Zaan in the Netherlands, and a story about Galfin's very clean restaurant. The restaurant had one small problem: Nobody was at the cash register.

Luckily, you never forget what's important. Right?

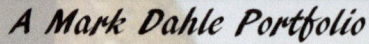

A Mark Dahle Portfolio

Farmer Jane

This Mark Dahle Portfolio includes a beautiful painting, twenty-five gorgeous photographs from the Netherlands, and a story about Farmer Jane.

Jane didn't know that farmers have troubles.

But she was about to discover how *many* troubles they have.